Queen Bee

Queen Bee

Discover Your Feminine Power!

Valerie Khoo

Red Wheel
Boston, MA / York Beach, ME

Contents

Introduction

Happiness, vitality, and a life that allows your dreams to come true may sound like a pretty tall order to some people. In fact, to many, this ideal existence may even seem impossible. But if you've picked up this book, you probably think that a life full of abundance, energy and joy is at least remotely possible. Well, you're right – it is. However, it's not some faraway dream – it's right there on your doorstep, waiting for you to grab it.

It all comes down to realizing that your dreams are there for the taking. Whether you have career aspirations, sporting goals, or a desire to improve your friendships and relationships, it all starts with a simple premise – that inside each and every one of us is an innate feminine power that can make things happen!

We're not talking about anything mystic or supernatural – just intrinsic powers that are nature's gift to every feminine soul. Inner strength, intellectual wealth, feminine intuition, and your personal spirituality are all natural resources within you. All you have to do is tap into them and bring them to the fore.

Take a look at the natural order of a beehive. Thousands of worker bees and drones perform their duties in service of one bee. It's the Queen Bee who seems to be getting all the goodies here. This bee, who unquestionably rules her domain, symbolizes all that we can become as powerful women. She has natural leadership ability – unlike other bees, she embodies an inner instinctive power.

We all have this power in us, but it often gets lost in among our hectic schedules, stressful jobs, challenging relationships and the busy business of living. We lose touch with our real potential and personal spirituality, and miss out on the incredible opportunities life has to offer us.

The Queen Bee is the guide for every woman who yearns to tap into her inner strength, confidence, and well-being. This book is about discovering your instinctive feminine power, and working out realistic, practical ways to make your dreams come true.

It will also take you on a journey of discovery. You will have fun and treat yourself like royalty along the way, and learn how to command a life full of abundance, joy and prosperity – a life that is fit for a Queen!

Who is the Queen Bee?

Are you a Queen Bee?

Of course you are! However, there are times when you may think your life doesn't even come close to the empowering existence of the Queen Bee. In fact, if you feel as if you're on a treadmill, you may even identify more with the worker bees – constantly working to please someone else, whether it's your boss, partner, or family.

Well, a wise woman once said that life wasn't meant to be easy. And she was right – our lives are often peppered with hard times and tough challenges. But the wise woman forgot to add that despite the twists and turns you discover on your path, you can still navigate your way through your life – you can achieve fulfilment and maintain your passion for living.

More importantly, you can design a life you're truly contented with by drawing on your innate strengths and unique talents and turning challenges into opportunities. But your dreams won't just fall into your lap while you sit around waiting for the world to dish up your wish-list of secret desires. Plum jobs, healthy bank balances and loving relationships don't appear at the wave of a magic wand. Whether you want to become the head of a company, find a career that excites you, or learn to play the cello, achieving your goals will take a little effort on your part.

Recognize the Queen Bee in Yourself

So how do you discover your Queen Bee instincts? You may already recognize some of them surfacing from time to time. Some women are more in touch with these instincts than others, but that doesn't mean their lives are any better or more successful. We all have the capacity to harness our innate strengths to help us get what we want out of life.

The key is to recognize when our personal Queen Bee resources are emerging – instead of repressing these natural instincts, we need to let this energy positively influence us.

SETTLING FOR LESS

Think about the times you feel your Queen Bee instincts rising, only to be suppressed or ignored. Have you ever found a stunning dress that's well designed and affordable, but perhaps just a little too stunning? Your instincts are saying, "You look amazing, you deserve it." But something else tells you it's a bit flashy and glamorous – and better left to someone with more confidence and chutzpah.

Instead of buying a beautiful outfit that's bound to make you look – and feel – like a Queen, you put it back on the rack. You may end up buying another dress, just so you don't feel like you're missing out. But it probably isn't nearly as beautiful as the first one. You've ignored your Queen Bee instincts and settled for second best.

9

GIVING IN TO GUILT

Your Queen Bee instincts are also at work in your social life. Let's say you're invited to a party with friends and would love to see them but you haven't had a day to yourself for weeks. Work commitments have meant your daily routine has consisted of waking up, spending all day in front of the computer, then going home to heat up a frozen dinner before crashing.

Even though your well-meaning friends try to convince you that some serious partying will be a good antidote, you know that all you want is a nice long bath, and an evening alone with your favorite book. Your instincts tell you this "me time" is essential, but you feel guilty for letting your friends down, so you ignore this inner voice and join your friends, only to feel 10 times more frazzled the next day.

KNOWING YOUR WORTH

There are many other instances where your Queen Bee instincts are repressed. Like when you know you've worked hard and deserve a promotion or pay rise, but feel it's too difficult to ask for one. Or perhaps you try, but settle for a raise that's not as much as you should be getting.

Have you ever found yourself at a seminar where the speaker inevitably concludes with "Any questions?" You hesitate to put your hand up because you don't want 600 people looking at you while you're trying to articulate your jumbled thoughts. Your instincts tell you it's a valid question and that getting a response from the speaker will help you a lot. These impulses nudge you to put your hand up – but your fear of embarrassment wins, and your Queen Bee is silenced.

SCARED OF SUCCESS

Similarly, you may desperately want to change your career or explore opportunities in an industry which has always captured your imagination. Perhaps you dream of starting your own business, or want to break into acting, or pursue a sport professionally. Your inner Queen Bee is ready and eager to go, but it is suppressed by a whole range of influences – well-meaning family and friends telling you that a secure job is better than a pipe dream, financial obstacles, or the simple fear of failure.

Recognizing your natural instincts and listening to what your Queen Bee is telling you is the first step to becoming more intuitive. You may think you're fairly in tune with this inner voice, but you need to do more than simply hear what's being said. You have to work out a realistic plan to turn these "words" into action.

HOW TO GET ROYAL TREATMENT

To nurture your Queen Bee instincts:

❀ Identify your role models. Write down the names of people you look up to, whether they're high-profile personalities or people in your own family. Figure out exactly what it is you admire about them and work to develop that character trait or talent in yourself.

❀ Remember exercise and nutrition. The combination of your mind, body and spirit is what makes you unique. If one area is worn out or deficient, the other areas have to work overtime to compensate. Looking after your body is vital if you want to tap into your natural energies and intuition.

❀ Surround yourself with positive people. Friends and family who encourage you to pursue your passions and achieve your goals are invaluable. Identify the members of your support group who will help you reach for your dreams.

❀ Develop your spirituality. Pay attention to your spiritual needs. This doesn't mean you suddenly need to go searching for a religion, but if or when you do feel the need to explore your spiritual side, follow this inner calling. You may be ready to discover something that can be very real, personal and soothing to your soul.

SUREFIRE WAYS TO STIFLE YOUR NATURAL INTUITION:

✿ Overloading your schedule. Handling work, family, hobbies and an enviable social life seems possible when you carefully schedule everything into your datebook. But rushing around and missing out on valuable time by yourself – to relax and regenerate – is guaranteed to repress your Queen Bee instincts.

✿ Listening to naysayers. You know the type. "As if you'll be able to start your own business in this market," they say. Or "Better keep ballet as a hobby, it's too tough to make it as a professional." People mean well, but if someone tries to discourage you, turn a deaf ear and shut the door. You're the only one who should shape your future.

✿ Thinking the glass is half empty. When you embark on a new phase of life, you can often be tempted to see all the things that could go wrong, instead of what could go right. Train yourself to see the benefits in new things, not the obstacles.

✿ Trying to do everything by yourself. Sometimes we can be so energized, we think we can do it all. But Queen Bees know they need to rely on the support of workers and drones to exist. Don't bust your arteries trying to take on everything on your own. If help is there to make life easier for you, use it!

But I don't want the Top Job!

Some of you may think you don't deserve to be Queen. Often, it's easy to say, "I just want a quiet life, I don't have big ambitions anyway," or "Life's hard enough as it is, I don't need this on my plate as well." But tapping into the Queen Bee inside you is easy – in fact, it's the most natural thing in the world.

It takes more energy to repress your instincts and innate gifts than it does to nurture them. If you give yourself the chance to explore your inherent strengths and capabilities, you'll be surprised how effortless it can be.

Or perhaps you're afraid of letting the Queen Bee inside you shine, because you don't want to be the focus of everyone's attention. Maybe

you're usually shy, the kind of person who would rather be in the background than the spotlight. Well, Queen Bees know that success is not about being in the limelight. It's about exuding a glow that's personally satisfying. This means that the only person you need to impress is yourself.

Maybe you don't want the top job because it sounds like too much hard work. Maybe you believe that making your dreams come true is something that only happens in Hollywood movies. It's like winning the lottery – there's only a one in a million chance that it will happen to you.

Well, before you even go down this road – stop! Once you let your natural instincts flow, and learn how to use some simple strategies to achieve your goals, you'll discover that it's far from hard work.

After all, you have a choice of making a difference, or doing nothing. You really don't have anything to lose – if you reach for something and don't make it, the worst that can happen is your situation will stay the same. On the other hand, you have the opportunity to gain a great deal.

So give yourself permission to create a life you'll love, especially when there is so much to gain for so little sacrifice. If you let her, your Queen Bee will help you soar.

Taking the First Step

It's simple. To take the first step, you don't have to pay money, join a program or sign up for a series of motivational tapes or videos. All you need to do is make a decision. There's no catch – it's as easy as that.

You need to make a decision that you're ready to nurture your inner Queen Bee so that you can live your life to its full potential. This means discovering your strengths and using them in practical ways to make your dreams become reality.

Although making a decision like this is easy, it's not something that should be taken lightly – you have to be making a firm commitment that you want your life to change for the better.

So now you're ready to work out a real plan, a strategy that will help you combine your dreams with practical actions, resulting in lasting change that will help you suck the nectar out of life.

The Nectar of Life

WHAT'S YOUR BUZZ?

Some of us dream big; others may have more modest aspirations. No matter which end of the spectrum you are at, your dreams are valid and important. Take Gina – she's a young woman climbing the corporate career ladder, and her ambition is to become a partner in her law firm by the time she's 30. Samantha is a budding fashion designer who dreams her label will make it big in Europe one day. And Kim is a young mother with two toddlers; she just wants to make it through the day and craves some time for herself.

Whether you're just starting your career, or already at the top of your industry, you have your own unique dreams and aspirations. And your goals may not have anything to do with high-flying career objectives; they

could be as simple – or obscure – as wanting to learn how to sew, or to climb the Eiffel Tower, or to pass a test to get a motor-bike license. No matter what your ambitions are, the first key is to identify them, so you can then embark on the exciting task of watching them come to fruition.

But I Have no Idea What I Really Want to Do!

Wat if you don't feel any burning desire to pursue anything in particular? Perhaps you know you're directionless, and have no idea what you really want to throw your energies into. Perhaps you can relate to laments like: "I know I can be really good at something … if I only knew what it was," or "I thought I'd figure out what I wanted to do by the time I grew up. Well, I'm grown up now and still haven't got a clue."

Well, this is where you can let your Queen Bee instincts guide your path. You don't have to create a lofty goal just for the sake of having something to aim for – after all, only dreams fueled by real passions are going to transform into reality. But see if you can let your innate strengths steer you in the direction of your true passions.

Firstly, figure out the kinds of activities or experiences you look forward to. What makes you excited? What would make you wake up with a spring in your step? It could be anything from listening to music or shopping to running marathons or simply going to the movies.

Remember, everyone's different. What rocks your world may seem totally mundane to someone else. Write down a list of five to ten activities or experiences you love.

Secondly, identify your skills and talents. Some of these skills may cross over into the first list, but others may be very different. For example, you may be fanatically interested in basketball but couldn't slam dunk to save your life. Similarly, you could have topped your class at med school but are actually passionate about creative writing.

Write down the skills you enjoy using and then see if you can align these skills with the interests you're passionate about from your first list. Some combinations may end up sounding ludicrous, but others may open your eyes to the possibilities of what can happen if you unite your passions with the talents you already have.

For example, Kaye is a 29-year-old high school geography teacher. This is how she worked through how to pursue her passions on a practical level.

KAYE

MY INTERESTS/PASSIONS

> Traveling the world
>
> Photography
>
> Saving the environment
>
> Kickboxing
>
> Any movie starring George Clooney

SKILLS/TALENTS I ENJOY USING

> Teaching and spending time with teenagers
>
> Can whip up a gourmet dinner party at short notice
>
> Winning the local trivia nights
>
> Decent amateur photography skills

HOW CAN I COMBINE MY SKILLS AND PASSIONS?

- Travel to Europe in the summer taking photos then see if any travel magazines are interested in buying them
- Coach kickboxing to teenagers
- Start a photography club for the kids at school
- Become president of the George Clooney fan club!
- Negotiate working three days a week so I can take photography more seriously — some people might even pay me!
- Start a sideline business organizing fundraising dinner parties cum trivia nights for local kickboxing groups or photography clubs
- Offer pro bono photography services for a "green" lobby group in exchange for being credited if any pictures are used in their publications.

Your Plan

Scan your own list and see which options appeal to you most. Remember, this list is not exhaustive. Keep thinking of different combinations till one captures your imagination. Let yourself be creative – write down all sorts of possibilities, then allow your instincts to guide you to the options you're most interested in.

In the end, Kaye worked out that she could just afford to live on a three-day-a-week salary, even though it would be a struggle. She decided to ask her employer if she could teach part-time so she could hone her photography skills and see if she could earn an income from it. The principal of the school agreed to trial a four-day working week – this gave Kaye the financial security of a steady income but freed up some time for her to develop her creative skills, market herself and score a few small photography jobs.

Some of you may already have clear goals in place and may not need to go through this process. However, we suggest giving it a go anyway. It's fun and you might come up with some viable options you hadn't considered before.

On the other hand, if you're looking for a bit of direction, this is an essential exercise – it can help you discover the range of paths available to you. These will be real alternatives that combine your interests and passions with the skills you already have.

Dreams of Life Beyond the Hive

Now that you've identified your goals, work out which ones you're going to concentrate on. Perhaps you're so enthusiastic that you now have a long list of aspirations. Once you've started on this journey it can be very exciting, and you may be tempted to take on more than you can actually handle.

But remember, you're unlikely to achieve much if you're running around trying to become a sought-after photographer who has a second career as a teacher, while competing at your local kickboxing championships, and throwing the odd dinner party on the days you're not volunteering for Greenpeace!

Slow down – although it's great to have a wide variety of interests, you don't want to multitask yourself to exhaustion. Be realistic and practical – it's best to concentrate on no more than three major goals at a time. This way, you can give each objective enough attention to make tangible changes and see real progress.

Now it's time to turn these visions into action.

How to Make It Happen!

Whether your dream is to become an opera singer, have a family or become CEO of a huge corporation, it can happen. Not straight away, but one day. And if you follow these practical strategies, that day will come sooner than you expect.

Remember, no one gets anywhere by sitting around waiting for things to happen. Whatever your dream is, the first thing you need to do is work out what you need to do to achieve it. It may sound very simplistic, but your aspirations can only be realized with a sensible concrete plan. This means breaking it down into little steps and working through the steps until your dream starts becoming a reality.

For example, if you've always dreamt of traveling across Europe and

Asia for a year, you'll need to research visa requirements, accommodation options, transport, and costs. You'll also need to budget, save regularly, and perhaps even consider asking your boss for a sabbatical year.

Write down a list of all the things you need to do to achieve your goal, being as specific as possible. This means it's not good enough to write "Save money" as one of the points on your list. Details are important. So write: "Open holiday savings account and transfer $50 per week into it."

Sue works in human resources but has always wanted to try a career in publishing.

<u>DREAM:</u> Get a job on a magazine

Break this down into steps and then into even smaller tasks:

DO A WRITING COURSE
- Find out if there any part-time courses offered by local colleges.
- Call a few magazines and ask which course they recommend.

GET ANY JOB ON A MAGAZINE AND MOVE INTO WRITING
- Track the employment pages each week for appropriate jobs.
- Post résumé on the Net.
- Write to a range of magazines in case some jobs aren't advertised.

FIND OUT MORE ABOUT HOW OTHER PEOPLE GOT INTO THE INDUSTRY
- Call features writers and ask for their advice.
- Ask my friends and see if they know anyone in the industry I can chat to.

GET PUBLISHED
- Find out if the local paper will accept contributions.
- Don't procrastinate! Devote one night a week to writing.
- Ask if I can write for my company newsletter.

Breaking your goals down into a series of "mini-goals" turns a big exercise into smaller, more manageable steps. If you can, break down your "mini-goals" even further, into tasks which take five or so minutes to complete. This way, you can tick one off each day, and before you know it, you're halfway through your list.

Overcoming Obstacles

Whenever we embark on any kind of change – big or small – a natural reaction is to see all the reasons why things should stay the same. That's because we're in a comfort zone which is familiar and unpredictable. Life may not be great, but it's not so bad either, so why rock the boat?

Are you already finding excuses? Reasons why it's too hard to do some of the tasks you've written down in the last section? If you are, take the time to break the tasks down into their simplest form, so they end up as easy, practical steps which are all achievable without too much effort.

If you believe your goals or dreams are just too big to break down into small steps, you're already putting obstacles in your own path – these need to be stomped on as soon as possible.

A Queen Bee is a practical being, and whether an obstacle is real or perceived, she can't just ignore it and hope it will go away. She has to deal with it. The most effective way to do this is to modify the way she approaches what's blocking her.

TURNING NEGATIVES INTO POSITIVES

Remember, the easiest thing to change is your attitude and your actions; this is much more practical than hoping external circumstances will some day align to suit your specific needs. Instead of seeing obstacles as overwhelming hurdles, turn them into positive actions that become part of your step-by-step series of "mini-goals."

Let's say you want to get a job in day care but you think: "That's impossible, because I'm trained as an accountant, and even though I love kids, I have no work experience looking after children." Turn that into "In order to get experience working with children I can volunteer at the day care center once a week, or help out at the day nursery in the local community hall."

TOO BUSY

NO EXPERIENCE

CAN'T AFFORD IT

Or perhaps you believe you can't work shorter hours to have extra time for studying or exploring another career because you have bills to pay and financial obligations that won't go away.

Obstacle: "I can't change my career because I can't afford it."

Action: "To see if my finances can support a career change, I need to visit a financial adviser to analyze my cashflow and find out the potential salaries of the jobs I'm interested in."

WHAT STEPS CAN I TAKE?

1. Contact a financial planners' association to get the name of an adviser in my local area.

2. Make an appointment with them.

3. Do a budget to see how much I spend each week/month.

4. Research salary prospects of new career on the Internet.

Once you transform your obstacles into positive actions and incorporate them into your list of "mini-goals," they start to become less of a barrier. When you progress through them, you may even be surprised that you considered them obstacles in the first place. Most importantly, turning these blocks into actionable tasks is a vital step in giving yourself permission to pursue your dreams.

You can shape your own future. If you don't, someone or something else will do it for you. And wouldn't you rather be in the driver's seat?

Remember, you can dream your life away, but your aspirations will stay firmly in your fantasies unless you actually bother to reach for them.

It sounds so simple that you probably think there's a catch. There isn't. Your dreams can come true – but only if you combine your aspirations with some real action.

Transforming into a Queen Bee
Your Inner Voice and Values

To truly harness your natural intuition and Queen Bee instincts, you need to do two vital things – listen to your inner voice and be clear on what your personal values are. Your inner voice is that "gut" feeling you sometimes experience, a natural sixth sense that may push you forward – or prevent you from heading in a particular direction.

Intuition is an intangible feeling that can subtly guide you – it is different from your values, which are personal beliefs that are much more defined. They are your principles or ethics, and they shape the way you think and act. Your values are based on what's important to you in your  life. They are deeply personal, and are unique to each person. No one except you should be measured according to your standards. Your values are the basis of many of your decisions – from how much to contribute for a co-worker's birthday present to how soon into a relationship you would sleep with your partner. Values guide you not only in any dilemmas you may find yourself in, but also in your day-to-day decisions.

An Authentic Life

Most importantly, your values help you lead a life where you're genuinely true to yourself. It may seem like a vague concept, so let's take a situation as simple as being invited to a wedding. Let's say the bride is your best friend's cousin and your best friend is the maid of honor. You haven't even met her cousin and you know the only reason you're invited is at the insistence of your best friend. Once again, you can choose not to go, but you know how excited your best friend has been about the dress, the shoes, the hair, everything. Even though she has a secondary role, it's still a big day for her.

So regardless of the fact that you don't even know the bride, you travel across the country to be there. That's because you value your relationship with your best friend and love seeing her happy – you know being there would mean a lot to her.

Now change this scenario. Say you've been invited to your old school friend's wedding. You're surprised to be on the guest list even though you did share a great friendship in the early years of high school. But when her family moved to the other side of the country, you slowly lost touch. Now, except for the occasional email, you don't have much in common at all.

This is where you have to listen to your intuition and look at your core values. Society teaches us to "do the right thing." We say yes because, quite simply, we want to be polite. "It's the most important day of her life," we say. But ask yourself honestly: do you really want to go? Would her day be ruined if you weren't one of the guests? The reality is that it probably wouldn't worry her if you couldn't make it.

And yet you may feel you should accept this invitation. This is where you need to assess your values. Say you value spending time with your family because you have a hectic work schedule that involves long hours at the office and precious little time at home. If so, will you resent the time away from your family and the money it will take to travel across the country and sit in a room full of strangers because of a girl you hardly know anymore?

Your core values should guide your decision – not what you think you "should" do – and if you end up declining the invitation, don't feel guilty. Go forward knowing you've been true to yourself.

Some decisions require minimal deliberation – this is generally when your initial response is closely aligned with your core values. However, if you're struggling with what choices to make, tap into your intuition and rely on your inner voice to guide you. It saves you a lot of time, because your decision-making yardstick is already in place to help you. Of course there are times when you will deviate from what this yardstick tells you, but at least it's there – you're never completely lost and confused about which way to go.

Who's in Your Hive?

Look at the kind of people who populate your life. Are you surrounded by supportive, positive friends, family, and colleagues?

In the office, you may not have much choice as to who your colleagues are – fortunately, some of us are blessed with fabulous workmates who are fun yet professional. When you're surrounded by proactive competent co-workers who behave with integrity, it can be empowering, and the day passes as a pleasure. Work buzzes along and you rarely find yourself looking at your watch, waiting for work to be over.

On the other hand, workmates can also be frustrating – indeed, they can even be a downright nightmare. What do you do when you have toxic office types who make your nine to five world less than ideal?

Short of changing jobs to get a new set of colleagues – which is a bit drastic – your best bet is to learn how to deal with these people. The key to dealing with toxic relationships at work comes back to your intuition and your core values. Base your decisions, comments and office friendships on what you've identified as important. This doesn't mean trying to impose any of your values on others; it just means not buying into their games.

Nurturing Friendships

The people you do choose to spend time with are a big influence on your life. If you find that hanging out with a particular friend – or group of friends – ends up making you feel bad, ask yourself why. Are they critical? Inconsiderate? Always in a bad mood and determined to bring you down with them.

Despite your bad feeling, it's unlikely that you will abandon your friends. That's because a natural Queen Bee instinct is to protect and nurture the people in her own hive – or life. And if these people are close to you, that's exactly what you need to do. Reach out, try to and see if there's anything behind this negativity – perhaps there's something troubling your friends, causing them to act this way.

However, if your friends think there's nothing wrong, that's when you need to talk to them about how their behavior makes your feel. Don't point out their faults – no one responds well to comments like "You know, you shouldn't criticize people so much," or "You sound really bitter when you say stuff like that." You may mean well, but your friends could take this as a personal attack, as if you believe there's something fundamentally wrong with them.

Focus on you, not them

Instead, concentrate on how you feel with comments like "I feel hurt when you tell me my clothes are out of date" or "I feel like I'm not very important to you when you always cancel on me at the last minute."

This approach is less of a criticism of their personal character because it focuses on your feelings, not their shortcomings. Remember, as a Queen Bee, give your friends the benefit of the doubt first, then – if you need to – approach them about how the negative aspects of the friendship impact on you. If they're a true friend, they're guaranteed to listen. If they don't, and your friendship doesn't look as if it's heading in a positive direction, take a long hard look at whether this person should be a significant part of your life. When you know you've done your best to nurture the friend-ship and it's still a cause of frustration, or sadness, it's healthier to minimize contact with this person than to continue exposing yourself to a negative attitude that won't change.

When to Use Your Sting!

By their very nature, Queen Bees are dignified creatures, but they are also strong and assertive. They're not afraid to use their sting and stand up for what's important.

But whether you're a man or a woman, if you want the respect of your peers and the inner contentment that comes with knowing you've behaved with integrity, you need to package your assertive and forthright manner with a little class.

Encouraging you to use your "sting" doesn't mean giving you a license to barge around like a bull in a china shop insisting that it's your way – or the highway. There's a big difference between being aggressive and being assertive.

Let's say you've just found out that your colleague has received a substantial pay rise even though she has exactly the same responsibilities as you. Regular worker bees may be tempted to storm into their boss' office and complain that the situation is unfair – which it is. Or they might just bitch to their friends about how the company determines salaries.

THE RIGHT APPROACH

A Queen Bee handles things with a bit more panache – and with more success. In this situation, you need to do your homework before you speak to your boss; you need to work out all the reasons why you deserve a pay rise and then prepare exactly what you're going to say. Your boss is far more likely to listen to you and ultimately remove the inequity if you calmly present a well-reasoned case. At the very least, you'll probably gain her respect for your professional approach to the situation.

Not everyone feels comfortable with being assertive, and for every woman who stands up for her rights, there's another who doesn't have the same strength or confidence. Some women would rather fade into the wallpaper than draw attention to themselves by being "forward." They've been conditioned not to rock the boat, and to believe that forcefulness isn't a "becoming" feature. When they don't stand up for what they want, it's often because, deep down, they don't think they deserve it.

It's a question of self-esteem, and this is not something that can be bolstered overnight. Perhaps you can't imagine yourself using your "sting" or fighting for what's right in this way. But as you allow your Queen Bee instincts to emerge, you'll slowly find yourself becoming more confident about being assertive. Remember, using your "sting" doesn't mean lashing out at or hurting anyone – it means drawing on your inner strength and resilience and standing up for what's important to you.

The Queen in Love

Discovering The Love Goddess Within

Queen Bees know that having a partner in love can mean an intimate and fulfilling relationship that involves sharing, trust and happiness. However, we often feel pressure from friends, family, or Tom Hanks and Meg Ryan movies, and feel that unless we're in a romantic relationship, there's something missing in our lives. Sometimes people embark on relationships for the wrong reasons, and end up frustrated or hurt.

Before you can be truly happy in a love relationship you need to be happy in yourself. It's a cliché we often hear, but it's true. It means living a life where you stay true to your values and give yourself the chance to pursue your passions. The first love you need to cultivate is a love for yourself, your life and your dreams.

This isn't a narcissistic arrogant self-love where you have to check yourself out in the mirror every two seconds, or gloat over your stash of sports trophies. It's a nurturing love that knows you need to become a "whole" person before you can successfully share yourself with another. If you don't achieve that, your energies will be used up nurturing someone else and your inner resources will be depleted till there is nothing left for you to draw on. The result can manifest itself physically – you may become run-down or stressed – or emotionally – being anxious, agitated, or depressed.

The first step in developing the love goddess within you is acknowledging that you don't need a partner to be happy. And that you have to

focus on making yourself happy before you can successfully build a relationship with someone else. You'll be surprised at how effective this attitude is – a confident, happy woman who loves life is much more attractive than someone who is obviously desperate to secure a partner.

Once you've acknowledged that loving yourself is a priority, it's good to also take steps toward achieving your goals and dreams – feeling yourself progressing on this journey and seeing your efforts come to fruition is a rewarding experience that will boost your confidence and passion for life. And a woman who exudes this zest for living is bound to attract a partner, like a bee to honey.

Avoiding The Wrong Drones

Sometimes, people we know are not good for us come into our lives. Often, though, there's something about them that is compellingly attractive. They're the bad boys who charm their way into our hearts but leave us bruised or broken when they ride off into the sunset. Think Pamela Anderson and Tommy Lee. Whitney Houston and Bobby Brown. Buffy and Angel.

And then there are the men who seem to have all the right credentials, but once you get close to them you start to see the darker side. I am not necessarily referring to men who are violent or abusive – if you ever find yourself in a relationship with one of these, get help and get out. These other men are almost as damaging, but on a more subtle level – they don't respect women, and so they are verbally abusive, neglectful, oppressive or controlling.

Unlike a bad boy, who makes no attempt to hide his heartbreaking intentions and wears his rebel badge planted clearly on his leather jacket,

these men are harder to spot. We often don't realize there's something wrong till deep into the relationship. So how do you spot the warning signs early on?

Be a Queen Bee – follow your values and stay true to what your intuition is telling you. If you feel you're involved with the wrong guy and should break up, short-term pain may be inevitable, but it's better than a lifetime of misery.

⋛ WARNING BELLS ⋚

How does he treat other women? Observe how he treats other women: his co-workers, sisters, and particularly his mother. If he doesn't respect the other women in his life – especially the ones in his family – how can you expect him to respect you?

Who controls your relationship? When we begin a new relationship, we are often very accommodating and more likely to compromise than usual. While this is certainly important, it's also vital to recognize whether you're being taken advantage of. Are you being so obliging that he relishes the control he has in the relationship? When you try reasserting your wants, is he uncomfortable sharing the reins?

Who are his friends and role models? You can tell a lot about a man by the company he keeps. If you don't get a good feeling from being around his friends, trust that intuition and investigate it. If it's just one or two you don't warm to, don't panic just yet – after all, you can't expect to get along famously with all his friends. But if more of them rub you the wrong way than not, think about whether he exhibits any of their unsavory traits.

Attracting a Partner, Like a Bee to Honey

Now you've managed to sift the bad boys out of your life, how do you go about attracting the kind of guy that is right for you?

Walk tall, walk proud: Consider the demeanor of any Queen – regal, poised, and self-assured. We're not saying you should stride around flicking the royal wave at all who pass, but think about how your physical disposition is a reflection of what's going on internally. Look at people who walk about as if they're studying the ground, who huddle into their coats as if to shut out the rest of the world, and appear so deep in thought that their gaze is transfixed on some distant point you can't even see. Body language like this screams: "I'm in my own world and you're not a part of it – do not disturb."

On the other hand, consider people who walk with purpose and yet maintain eye contact and an open, friendly demeanor. Apart from appearing happier and more approachable, when you walk with your head high and your eyes taking in the scene in front of you, you're better able to pick up on what's going on around you. Regardless of the fact that it increases your attraction quotient, it just makes sense to have a greater level of awareness of the people and circumstances affecting you rather than to stay hunched in your own little world.

Expect and insist on royal treatment: We're not suggesting you expect your suitors to kowtow to you and submit to all your wishes. Such an unbalanced partnership would be destined for failure. Nor does it mean that your partner should constantly shower you with expensive gifts. "Royal treatment" has nothing to do with money – it's about being treated with the respect you deserve.

Naturally, this works both ways. You can only expect respect if you earn it, and if you bestow it on those around you – your friends, family, colleagues, and, of course, your partner. But if you allow yourself to be walked over, and you submit to less than ideal treatment, you're setting a low benchmark for your relationship. Expect the best, offer the best yourself, and don't settle for less.

The beauty Queen: One of the fundamental elements of Queen Bee attraction is to look and feel like royalty. This doesn't mean you need to take hours to do your makeup, pore over what to wear, and make sure your

hair is styled to within an inch of its life in order to attract the right man. Far from it – you just need to pay attention to whatever's going to make you feel confident and gorgeous.

Put simply, wanting to look good and feel great should be about making you comfortable

43

and bolstering your self-esteem. If this is your focus, the flow-on effect is that you'll exude a poised assurance that is always attractive to others. So if getting your hair done is a treat, or wearing your favorite shade of lip gloss makes you feel like a million bucks, go for it.

Do whatever it is that's going to make you feel better about yourself – it's a tiny effort for a big payoff.

THE SEXY SIDE OF BEING QUEEN

All Queen Bees know that a fundamental part of being a woman is being able to explore and nurture our sensuality. We are sexual beings, and one important aspect of love and romance is being able to give and experience pleasure. This means being in touch with our senses and enjoying different aspects of our sexuality.

However, you don't have to wait for a man to come along to do this. In fact the more attuned you are with this side of your nature, the more likely it is that you're going to enjoy yourself when you're sharing the experience with someone else.

Sensuality doesn't necessarily mean lacy lingerie, bedroom banter and love-making sessions that last long into the night. Exploring your sensuality simply means heightening your sensual awareness and allowing yourself to really feel, touch, smell, hear, and see – and above all appreciate and indulge in – everything around you.

It can involve something as simple as delicious food enjoyed in a candlelit room with soft music playing in the background. Most people associate this picture with a romantic date for two, but who says this beautiful setting needs to be reserved for a couple? Why not enjoy it even when you're alone?

Similarly, don't reserve your silk sheets or beautiful lingerie for when you have company. If wearing them makes you feel great, put them on!

Why wear your frayed flannel pajamas when you could be indulging in something far more beautiful? Perhaps you think they should be saved for a special occasion. But why wait when you can turn every day into a series of small indulgences?

And if you've got gorgeous underwear that you usually save for certain occasions or outfits, get it out from the back of the drawer and wear it. Who cares if it's hidden under your work clothes – you'll know it's on and it'll make you feel great. Don't wait for a partner to be in your life before you enjoy all things sexy. Start now – you'll look great and feel fantastic.

Simply Sensual — With or Without a Partner

These are easy things you can do to help you experience more pleasure from your day-to-day living:

* Light candles around your house, play your latest (or favorite) CD and indulge in your favorite meal.
* Sleep in the nude.
* Buy matching bra and panties and wear them.
* Revamp your sleepwear wardrobe – throw out all the T-shirts you've been using as pajamas and buy some gorgeous lingerie.
* Wear your favorite fragrance at home, even when you're not expecting visitors
* Have a bath with rose petals and essential oils.
* Enjoy sexy underwear under your conservative work clothes – you'll feel great all day.
* Wear a nice outfit even if you're at home – just because you're by yourself doesn't mean you shouldn't look attractive.

Making Relationships Work

Communication: One of the biggest obstacles to developing open and effective communication in a relationship is when partners have differing expectations and don't convey them to the other person. Instead, they presume their partners know what they want. Unless you've been anointed with a cosmic mind-reading power, this is not going to work.

Often, we're too caught up in the heady feeling of being in love to bother with the details. A lack of communication leads to assumptions, which result in a gap in expectations. Unless this is cleared up, someone is likely to end up disappointed. It's important to be able to talk openly, honestly – and tactfully – about anything, from what you want for dinner to your plans for the future.

Compromise: Working alongside effective communication is the ability to compromise. While it's essential to be able to voice your wants and needs, it's equally important to understand that no relationship works unless both partners are willing to give and take. This is where the core Queen Bee values you identified in Chapter 3 will guide you. The ones at the top of the list may involve issues you'll rarely compromise on – you may have a strong religious faith, for example, and feel it's important that your partner supports those beliefs. On the other hand, there may be areas where you're prepared to give a little more. For example, perhaps you come from a strict vegetarian household but are willing to compromise on this so that your partner can cook meat at home.

Commitment: This is the glue which binds successful relationships, because when the initial sparks fade, and the day-to-day process of living together becomes routine, it's your commitment to each other which is going to keep your passion for each other burning. And that's exactly what love is about.

Love may be a wonderful feeling that gives you a warm glow when you think of your partner, and it can be that intoxicating rush that makes you find him irresistible, but most of all, true love comes down to a decision – an intentional choice – to commit to a partnership.

Busy Bees at Work
Give Yourself Permission to Shine

To be successful at work – whether that means making money, scoring promotions or simply loving what you do – you need to dare to be different. That doesn't mean growing a third head, or creating attention-stealing scenes that scream "Look at me" every five seconds. The differences may be subtle, but they are what will set you apart from the rest of the pack. And as a Queen Bee, you need to give yourself permission to embrace the limelight from time to time. More importantly, you need to be proactive about cultivating your talents and making sure the right people are aware of your assets.

A DIFFERENT WORLD

Older generations were generally taught that if they worked hard and stayed loyal to a company, they would progress steadily up the ranks, and the inevitable gold watch would be presented upon retirement. But working life is now light years away from that concept. Few of us will stay with the same company all our lives, and many will change careers several times before finding our true calling.

The rise of project-oriented work and the increase in people entering new careers later in life mean that employers don't have the pool of loyal, steadfast talent they once had. Instead, the faces in the job pool aren't as familiar as they used to be, and they come from a range of diverse backgrounds. If you want to be Queen Bee at work you need to stand out and promote your unique skills.

Do accept praise or compliments, especially when you've worked hard and your boss or colleagues are acknowledging your efforts with a genuine pat on the back. Don't be self-effacing and mumble, "Oh it really wasn't that hard, anyone could've done it" when someone congratulates you on a job well done. Accept and appreciate the compliment and simply say, "Thanks."

However, you also need to know the difference between exuding a confident glow and arrogantly boasting about your achievements. No prizes for guessing which characteristic will earn you the most respect. Downplaying your achievements is bad, but gloating about your efforts won't win you any fans. You need to be proud of your achievements without going over the top.

IDENTIFY YOUR ASSETS

Most people know their Queen Bee is just waiting to shine at work. How many times have you heard people say: "I know I can do that job, I'm just not sure how to get there" or "I know I want to start a business, I just don't know what it is yet." And yet these same people see others – with similar skills, talents, and opportunities – on a fast track to the top while they're still struggling to get past go.

It's not your level of skill or a particular personality trait that will determine your success – it's what you do with these assets. If you hide your talents, downplay your abilities and are constantly so self-deprecating that you convince others you're not as good as you really are, you're clearly going to move at a much slower pace than someone who is proud of their skills.

Whether or not getting ahead in your career is one of your ambitions, nurturing your talents and knowing the unique characteristics that make up "you" is a rewarding process – even if you're the only one you're showing off to. Figuring out what sets you apart, what makes you special, is also good for your self-esteem. It's a process that helps you realize the things that make you who you are.

DON'T BE LIMITED BY YOUR CURRENT ROLE

Just because you have a title – whether it's manager, salesperson, or dental nurse – doesn't mean you need to be limited to this role and set of responsibilities. You're now not only Queen; you've also elected yourself President of Me Inc, a brand that needs to be marketed, improved and promoted. Go beyond what's expected of you and show people you're capable of more – they'll notice.

WHO'S YOUR AUDIENCE?

While it's important that people be aware of your achievements, you need to ensure that this is done in the right way. Don't march into your boss' office each afternoon to tell her how much you've accomplished, and don't send regular group emails to your colleagues force-feeding them information about your successes.

Do network with your superiors, peers, and subordinates – and maintain genuine relationships through which your achievements can be noticed. This involves more than forwarding every email joke you get in your inbox to your office address list. Peers and subordinates are very important in this equation, because they can help market you too, especially when the conversation around the watercooler turns to who may be good to recommend for an upcoming opportunity.

Finally, don't promote yourself by citing someone else's shortcomings or failure – it's tacky and unprofessional.

CREATING HARMONY IN YOUR HIVE

Getting along with your colleagues is important in fostering a productive environment, and a peaceful workplace. We already know that when confronted by less than ideal workmates, we need to rely on our core values to guide us. Now let's look at specific examples of how we can deal with common toxic types who can turn our work day into a battle zone.

The bitch: This is the woman who honed her skills studying Amanda from Melrose Place. She makes life hell at work, bullies her staff and doesn't care who she squashes as long as she gets the job done and is advancing her career. The first thing you need to figure out is whether she's being a bitch to you, or a tyrant to anyone and everyone who happens to be nearby.

If you're not the one who is specifically under attack, then obviously she's just good at spreading her toxic influence around. The key is to remember that it's not personal. Try to take a "water off a duck's back" approach – after all, it's a lot easier to try to change your attitude to the situation than to attempt to change her malicious ways.

On the other hand, if you find that she's directing her venom particularly at you, you need to deal with the situation – with kid gloves. It's important to find out the reason for the attack; there may be some kind of misunderstanding or unresolved issue behind it all. Perhaps invite her for a chat or coffee, somewhere out of the office and on neutral ground, where you can discuss the matter without being in a negative environment. If she insists there's no issue to discuss, perhaps your personalities simply clash.

This is certainly no excuse for bad behavior, but if it's the problem, you need to rise above it. Let your regal Queen Bee instincts guide you toward being civil and professional. Don't go out of your way to be best friends with her, but don't give her any reason to treat you with spite. You'll show her up for being a bitch, and other people will eventually see what's going on and respect you for your dignified approach.

The slacker: This is the guy or girl who is most likely to be found gossiping around the watercooler, out to yet another long lunch, or who has called in sick for the day. Meanwhile, as this person's colleague, you've been left to pick up the slack and cover for his or her laziness.

To entice this sort of person away from surfing the Net all day or chatting to friends on the phone, there needs to be something in it for them – people like this are most likely to respond to suggestions if they're going to benefit in some way. Let's say you have a big project due, and you know it is going to require some long hours at the office. Approach the situation by saying something like, "I know we've got to get a lot done, but I'm happy to stay late to help you out if you like." Sound as if you're doing the person a favor and they'll probably take advantage of it. So think about what's going to appeal to their slacker nature and develop a strategy which makes it seem that as if they'll gain from your suggestion.

The gossip: Unlike the bitch, the gossip usually doesn't have any malicious intentions. She simply loves to chat. The trouble is, her gossip has a way of being embellished each time she retells a story – and unlike chat about who's dating who in Hollywood, which doesn't affect the real lives of any of us, her chat is invariably about the people we work with. Whether you're the chief executive or the mail room boy, she doesn't

discriminate when it comes to good gossip fodder, and no one is immune from starring in one of her tall stories.

How do you handle this situation? Simple. Tell her nothing: don't reveal anything about your personal life and don't share your career aspirations or frustrations with her – you can be sure that whatever you say will have made the rounds of the office before you've even had time to return to your desk. That's not to say you should shun these people – they're actually fairly harmless. They just doesn't know when to keep their mouths shut. Play your cards close to your chest, don't spread any gossip to them yourself, and simply listen. The less you talk, the more they'll gab on, and you might even discover a thing or two – at the very least you've got some guaranteed entertainment while you're waiting for the photo-copier to warm up.

Pursuing Your Passions

One of the most satisfying things in life is to be able to truly say that you love your work. Some people certainly "like" what they do, others "don't mind" it, and yet others "hate every minute" on the job. Sadly, there are precious few individuals who are able to say they are passionate about their career.

Your journey of transformation from a regular worker bee to a Queen means you need to identify your passions, and you then need to pursue them and shape your career until you're getting paid for doing what you love.

Many people believe that to pursue your dreams you need to forego a secure financial future, give up a hefty salary, or live like a starving artist while you chase something that may or may not work. This myth is perpetuated by those who are too scared to follow their hearts and make their dreams come true. You definitely don't have to sacrifice your life savings in order to pursue your goals.

TAKE A CHANCE

Admittedly, it can be intimidating to venture away from a secure job and into something unknown and new, but it's at least worth investigating. That first step often seems insurmountable, and you're likely to put it in the "too hard" basket, with the intention of tackling it later. But once that step is finally made, people wonder why they didn't take it sooner.

Many people don't contemplate switching careers because they are not prepared to make a financial sacrifice. However, this sacrifice may be

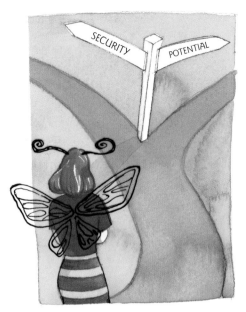

short-lived and not too dramatic if you follow the portfolio career approach outlined in the next section. If you love what you do, you'll not only enjoy work more, you'll be constantly honing your skills and developing your expertise. Therefore, opportunities – and financial rewards – will follow.

Wouldn't it be great to wake up each day knowing you're going to enjoy your work? There's nothing more rewarding than getting a genuine buzz out of your job and feeling like pinching yourself to make sure you're really awake – because you can't believe you're being paid for doing what you love.

Remember, the main difference between someone who turns her dreams into reality and someone who doesn't is simply that one of them bothered to try.

Portfolio Careers

If you're thinking of transitioning to another career, but the jump just seems too scary, you might consider an approach many people are embracing these days – a portfolio career. This is where you have one or more income-producing careers going at the same time. For example, Julie-anne is a food stylist, but she also teaches aerobics three times a week. Similarly, Suzanne is a graphic designer who runs a small catering business on weekends. And Cathy has three "careers" going at once: she's a primary school teacher, a wedding photographer, and also makes money from writing and selling short stories.

Portfolio careers have risen in popularity for a number of reasons. First, with the "one company for life" concept disappearing, plus corporate collapses, factory closures and constant downsizing, people are becoming used to the idea of needing a more non-traditional approach to their working life. Second, more people are realizing that it is possible to pursue more than one career at a time. As increasing numbers of people adopt this approach, we see that it can work. It also makes sense.

DIVERSIFY YOURSELF

Think about the way you've been taught to invest your financial assets. To lower risk, advisers suggest diversifying your investments, so that all your eggs aren't in the one basket. Why should your career – one of your most valuable assets – be any different?

Pursuing different options means you have variety – many people combine a "traditional" career, such as law, management, or accounting, with something perceived as a bit more creative. It also makes sense in that if one area slumps, you have an alternative to fall back on.

The trouble is, we're often taught to concentrate our efforts in one particular area. For years, careers counselors told us to specialize and create a niche where we'll be in demand. While this is fine for some people, others crave flexibility and diversity, and don't want to be pigeonholed into one industry or job. Portfolio careers are useful if you simply love the idea of a multiplicity of career options, but they are also appropriate if you want to move from one career to another. If you pursue both the old and the new at the same time, you can test the waters in your new career without sacrificing all the security and familiarity of the old one.

Body and Soul

HEALTH AND VITALITY

To be able to tap into your unique Queen Bee instincts, it's essential that you give your body royal treatment. This means maintaining a healthy lifestyle that will help you glow with confidence and fuel you with the energy you need to live life to the full.

Treating your body with the respect it deserves involves two main aspects – ensuring that you're nourishing it with a balanced diet, and keeping it healthy and in good working order through appropriate exercise and activity. This may sound as if we're talking about some kind of machine, and that's exactly how we should be thinking about our bodies – but our body is much more complex than a machine: it's a living, breathing organism which needs to stay with us for, well, a lifetime. It's vital to maintain it, because it's the only one we'll ever have.

Fabulous fare

Some people see the words "healthy lifestyle" and immediately think this means a diet of carrot sticks, grueling gym sessions, and a dry, teetotal existence. But you don't have to adopt this spartan way of life in order to shine with vitality. In fact, far from it. Queen Bees know that embracing the abundance life offers means being able to experience and enjoy everything that's available. The key is to enjoy everything in moderation.

Nourishing your body involves having a balanced diet that provides you with all the nutrients you need. Deprive yourself in one area, such as vegetables, or over-indulge in another, such as carbohydrates, and your body will compensate for the nutritional imbalance in some way – you may feel sluggish, be more susceptible to viruses, or put on weight.

If you sustain a regular, balanced diet – with the fundamental premise being one of moderation – then even the occasional over-indulgence will be okay.

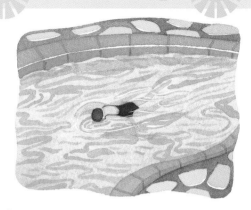

GET ENERGIZED!

You also need to apply this commonsense approach to your levels of exercise. If you're already involved in an active lifestyle, keep it up! When you're fit and healthy you feel energized – your body and mind both work better. However, if you've never been a big fan of exercise, don't think you have to suddenly transform yourself into an aerobics junkie or go jogging at the crack of dawn, particularly if the thought of these activities fills you with dread. But do consider developing an exercise program you will enjoy – filled with active pursuits you'll find interesting.

We're all motivated by different things: while your best friend may love golf, you may think it's the most tedious game on the planet. And while some people can swim endless laps of the pool with nothing but the black line on the pool floor to keep them company, others prefer team sports where they can interact with others. The trouble is, many of us punish ourselves with exercise we simply don't enjoy. If that's the case, stop! Invest your time and energy in exploring activities you haven't sampled yet – you may find one you love. Whether it's kayaking, yoga, martial arts or simply walking the dog, regular exercise will give you renewed zest and vigor. Once you incorporate it as an integral part of your lifestyle you'll wonder how you ever lived without it.

The Right Motivation

Every day, we're bombarded with images of women – in magazines and on television – who are considered beautiful, successful, or attractive. Most of these women are very thin – indeed some models are so skinny they're nothing but a delicate layer of skin holding up a collection of bones.

There's nothing wrong with being thin. But aspiring to being skinny should definitely not be the focus of your efforts – your goal should be to be healthy, and to treat your body with respect. Glowing with vitality and having the energy to pursue all the things you want in life is a goal you're more likely to achieve and maintain than merely dropping a dress size.

Sure, crash diets and intense periods of exercise may give you short-term results, but they are gains that will disappear as soon as you go back to your normal routine. Unless you make changes to your day-to-day

lifestyle, you'll find it a constant battle to be healthy. But once you begin incorporating small changes into your life – even things as simple as eating fruit every day or walking instead of catching the bus – you'll notice a difference. Your efforts to be healthy won't seem like a chore; they'll be a pleasure.

Buzzing with Activity

In today's fast-paced world, you may sometimes feel you're doing too many things at once. Juggling a career, social life, perhaps part-time study, and the demands of your family, is often difficult – and one tiny bump can send everything flying off the rails. But one essential part of being Queen Bee is to take time out for yourself – to relax and be alone with nothing but your thoughts and dreams for company.

If you don't take some time out to renew your mind and refresh your soul, you'll end up run-down and worn out. To let your Queen Bee instincts work to their full potential, it's critical to schedule in this vital "Me-time."

Me-time: Finding Time for Yourself in a Pressure-Cooker World

❀ Schedule time in your diary. Block off a period of your day, even if it's just an hour, and use this to be alone to do whatever you want — whether it's reading a book, doing your nails or just listening to music while lying on your sofa.

❀ Chill out before bed. Perhaps you have a habit of reading your favorite crime fiction or watching the late news before you turn the light off. Instead, try to find at least 10 to 20 minutes before bedtime where you put on soothing music, empty your thoughts and breathe slowly till you're in relaxed state. You'll have a great sleep.

❀ Treat yourself. If you're the kind of person who always has people around and wouldn't know what to do with yourself if you had to spend time alone, turn the experience into a luxury. Set aside half a day for pampering — give yourself a facial, buy an aromatic body lotion and indulge in a foot massage. Then put on your favorite video or DVD, and enjoy.

❀ Go outside. For those who prefer the great outdoors, you could go hiking, walking along the beach or simply sitting on a rock watching the world pass you by. With the sun on your back and a breeze on your face, this therapeutic Me-time can revitalize your soul after a busy week.

❀ Write in a diary or journal. The process of writing down your thoughts or frustrations can be a great release. If you don't like the idea of putting your deepest secrets on paper, consider writing a "thank" diary instead, simply listing anything from scoring a promotion to discovering a café with the most delicious burger this side of town. This helps you focus on the positive things happening in your life — big or small.

Tackling Life's Bumps and Bends

As we all know, life isn't always a bed of roses. Sometimes we're faced with challenges and obstacles we could do without. One essential part of the being a true Queen Bee is knowing when to ask for help, and understanding that you don't have to tackle your problems all alone.

Even in her hive, the Queen Bee is constantly assisted by workers and drones – a host of helpers whose sole aim is to make her life easier. Why should your life be any different? Not only is it harder to face difficulties without the support of friends or advisers, but you'll also spend more time than you need to recovering from any hiccups.

Although other people can't solve your problems for you, nor magically take away any pain or sadness you may encounter, their support, encouragement, and guidance can make a big difference. And while it's important to rely on friends and family for these things, your close network of supporters can be a bit too close to help with certain issues.

Even if you have good friends, you may still feel very alone if you're not comfortable talking to them about your concerns. So see if there is a professional counselor, psychologist, or coach who may be able to guide you through your situation.

Professional advisers aren't personally involved, and can often help you with objective advice – at the very least they may make it easier for you to see your situation from a different perspective. However, it's also important to note that not all professional advisers may suit your specific needs and personality. If you find the first one you go to is of no benefit, this doesn't mean you've failed in any way, or that that person was not competent. It's like shopping – just find another one that suits you better.

Work out what kind of adviser is best for your particular needs – a careers counselor, psychotherapist, life coach, relationships counselor, lifestyle strategist, spiritual adviser or even personal trainer. They won't have all the answers, but they can help you head in the right direction.

Everyday Rituals for All Queen Bees

Every day ...

- ❀ Commit to living your day staying true to your values.
- ❀ Trust your intuition and follow what your instincts are telling you.
- ❀ Do one small thing that will bring you a step closer to achieving your goals or dreams.
- ❀ Respect your body and focus on your health and vitality.
- ❀ Take time out from your hectic schedule so you can relax, de-stress and renew your physical and mental energy.
- ❀ Encourage and support others to reach for the stars – they'll do the same for you.

Make Your Life as Sweet as Honey
PROSPERITY AND ABUNDANCE

Queen Bees know that a life of prosperity and abundance is at their fingertips. But like most things, wealth won't simply appear out of nowhere. You need to take some practical steps, and, most importantly, to understand that the only person who can make a real difference to your financial affairs is you.

Many of us think that financial planning is a complicated process, but it's not. It just takes a little bit of common sense.

I NEVER SEEM TO HAVE ENOUGH MONEY!

One complaint we all have is that we never seem to have enough money. There are bills to pay, and unexpected expenses that eat into the bank balance, and somehow even those of us who are not spendthrifts end up with a lot less in our purses than we planned.

This isn't some spooky unexplained phenomenon. There are no gremlins that raid your wallet as you sleep each night and your credit cards don't go sneaking out to the mall by themselves. It's as basic as this: you spend more than you intend to. If this keeps up, you will find it a battle to save, and, in extreme cases, you may be in danger of spiraling into a real debt problem.

They key is to budget, and to use a few tricks that'll help you keep your cash flowing in, not out.

The Queen Bee Rules of Managing Your Cash

Budget – Work out what your expenses are – mortgage/rent, food, transport, entertainment, and other costs. It's not hard; if you take 20 minutes now, you'll probably have it completed. Are there areas where you're over-spending? Once you've worked out your budget, stick to it. That means if you've already used your budgeted funds for entertainment in a particular week, you know you have to either forego the theater tickets you hoped to buy, do something cheaper, or wait till you can use next week's entertainment allocation.

Save – Some people think saving is a waste of time; they would rather spend their money on enjoying life right now. But putting away even just a small amount every week or month is a great habit to cultivate. To make it easy, figure out a set amount that you are going to save each month and make sure it goes immediately into a separate bank account. Make sure this bank account isn't readily accessible – don't activate Internet transfer or ATM access options. When sufficient funds accumulate, put it in a term deposit.

Resist temptation – Keeping your ATM card in your wallet is one of the easiest ways of letting your money slip through your fingers. If you don't have a lot of discipline with your cash, put your weekly budget into your wallet and live off it for the week. Once the cash starts dwindling, you know you need to watch where it's going. Don't replenish the cash until the following week, and don't allow yourself to withdraw anything from the bank.

Credit cards – Similarly, credit cards can almost seem like free money. It's tempting to spend, but you will be faced with an ugly bill at the end of your spree. It's easy to fall into the credit card trap – if you find yourself struggling to make just the minimum payment every month, you need to take drastic action as soon as possible. If you don't, the interest rates will soon see you owing much more than you bargained for. Don't charge anything else to your card until it's reached a zero balance, and consider paying off your credit with a loan that has a lower interest rate than the rate being charged on the credit card.

Invest wisely – Once you get a little nest egg going, even just $1000, don't let it sit there in a low-interest bank account. Find a financial product that will give you a higher return, such as term deposits or cash management accounts, or consider investing in a share portfolio or managed fund.

The right advice – Don't be afraid to ask for help. Visit a financial adviser to see what options you have. Remember, you don't have to follow their advice – you're under no obligation to open any new accounts or invest in what they suggest – but at least you will be more aware of the options available.

It's the little things – You might think you live a fairly frugal existence, but it's often the little things that end up making a big impact on your finances. Like the magazines you purchase and never end up reading, or the lattes you buy in the afternoon even though there's a free coffee machine in the office. Ask yourself if you really need all these "little things" – you'll be surprised at how much you'll end up saving if you give up even one of them.

The Queen at Home

Your home is your sanctuary, and whether you're in your own apartment, sharing with others, or living with your family, your home should be your little slice of heaven. So it's important to keep it feeling both vibrant and energized, so that it inspires you, and cozy and comfortable enough for you to relax in.

This doesn't mean you need to hire Martha Stewart to come over and decorate, but it does mean turning your home into a livable, functional, enjoyable place to spend time in. If you're still living with your family, you may not have much say on the rest of the house, so treat your room like your own "home" instead.

TURN YOUR HOUSE INTO A HOME – NOW!

Often, we delay beautifying our surroundings with excuses like "When I have my own apartment, I'll hang up all my paintings," or "If I had more books, I'd buy a decent bookshelf," or "I won't buy anything nice, because I'm only here temporarily."

While these excuses are sometimes valid, we often end up staying put longer than we initially expected to – once we're settled into a place, moving is no longer a priority. So two years later, we haven't hung our favorite pictures on the wall, there are still-packed boxes hidden under the bed, and we haven't bothered to delete the last resident's name from the doorbell. Over a lifetime, we're likely to move around fairly often, so it's important that we transform each place into somewhere we feel safe, comfortable and completely free to be ourselves. Here are a few ways you can turn your address into a home:

Make it uniquely yours: Turn your place into somewhere that's cozy and familiar by sticking photos on the fridge, hanging up your favorite pictures, and placing knick-knacks or mementos on your shelves. Combine this with new pieces of furniture – or even smaller items such as candles or vases – to lift your place with something new and refreshing.

Color: The color of your walls and the things that surround you can make a big difference to your moods and the overall atmosphere of your home. Vibrant colors such as red, orange, and yellow energize a room and provide an invigorating warmth. However, these colors may not be appropriate for a room where you want a relaxing, soothing environment. Here, calmer colors such as muted blues, greens and pastels can work better. Check out the hues that currently surround you, and have fun coloring your world.

Clearing your space: If there's one thing you can do to increase the harmony of your home, it's to declutter. Perhaps there's a stack of magazines in the corner of the room you haven't even touched since you bought them, or maybe you have a stash of 20 tea towels – some of which should have been thrown out years ago. Or possibly your wardrobe is bursting with clothes you've had for years but never wear, ones you're hanging on to in the hope that they'll be fashionable again any day now. Culling your possessions doesn't mean you need to live a minimalist existence, but freeing up your physical space will do more than give you a more livable environment – it will also help declutter your mind.

Declutter Checklist:

Spend a day – or however long it takes – getting rid of everything you don't need:

❀ Donate old clothes to a local charity or give them away to your friends.

❀ Take unwanted books and magazines to a second-hand dealer. If there isn't one near you, see if your local library wants them.

❀ Hold a garage sale to sell off ornaments and furniture you don't need; you may even make some extra cash.

❀ If something's broken – whether it's your coffee table, television, or a wristwatch – fix it or ditch it.

❀ Sort through old photos, and keep only the ones you like – in an album. Perhaps you can even scan them, so that you always have them but don't need to worry about storing negatives.

❀ Collect all your paperwork – the bills, insurance policies, car registrations papers, and receipts – and keep it all in one place, not strewn in every drawer in the house.

❀ Always keep your bedroom clutter-free. If you're a natural hoarder, try to confine your collections anywhere but your place of rest, because cluttered environments aren't conducive to a peaceful sleep. And Queen Bees need their sleep.

HOW TO BE THE BEST-EVER QUEEN

The main result of allowing your innate Queen Bee instincts to guide you in life is a genuine contentment – you will be living true to your personal values and tapping your full potential. These instincts not only help you make decisions and determine your path, they'll also inspire and encourage you to reach for your goals and make your dreams come true. You just need to let these instincts flow, to nurture them so that they become part of your day-to-day living.

But remember, you need more than just this innate resource to make things happen. Your instincts need to be combined with action – practical steps that turn visions into reality. Your ideal life won't appear by magic;

it takes a step-by-step plan, a positive attitude and the ability to turn obstacles into opportunities.

It's there waiting for you – a life of abundance, joy, and prosperity that's fit for a Queen. A personally exhilarating and rewarding life is not some remote possibility that might happen one day if your planets align. It's already there on your doorstep. Take all the wonderful things life has to offer, give yourself the respect you deserve, and encourage others in their personal aspirations.

Let your natural instincts guide you, follow your passions, and, most importantly, give yourself permission to live your dreams, and you'll be on the path toward a magnificent life. Enjoy!

Published in 2002 by Lansdowne Publishing Pty Ltd
Level 1, 18 Argyle Street, Sydney NSW 2000, Australia

First published in the United States in 2002 by
Red Wheel/Weiser LLC
York Beach, ME
With offices at:
368 Congress Street
Boston, MA 02210
www.redwheelweiser.com

Commissioned by Deborah Nixon
Text: Valerie Khoo
Illustrations: Sue Ninham
Design: Sue Rawkins
Copy Editor: Sarah Shrubb
Production Manager: Sally Stokes
Project Coordinator: Kate Merrifield

ISBN 1-59003-041-9

This book is intended to give general information only. The publishers expressly disclaim
all liability to any person arising directly or indirectly from the use of, or for any errors or
omissions in, the information in this book. The adoption and application of the information
in this book is at the reader's discretion and is his or her sole responsibility.

Set in Goudy and Girls are Weird on QuarkXPress
Printed in Singapore by Tien Wah Press (Pte) Ltd

08 07 06 05 04 03 02
 7 6 5 4 3 2 1

The paper used in this publication meets the minimum requirements of the American
National Standard for Information Sciences—Permanence of Paper for Printed Library
Materials Z39.48-1992 (R1997).